Alison Gardner

Crabtree Publishing Company
www.crabtreebooks.com

Author: Alison Gardner
Editor: Crystal Sikkens
Project coordinator: Kathy Middleton
Production coordinator: Ken Wright
Prepress technician: Margaret Amy Salter
Series consultant: Gill Matthews

Picture credits:
Corbis: Robert Holmes 11, Christian Liewig/Tempsport 18c
Istockphoto: Leon Bonaventura throughout,
  Ilker Canikligil 10c, Michael DeLeon 8t,
  Yury Khupchenko 6, Michel Mory 7t
Rex Features: Sipa Press 9t
Shutterstock: (Cover), Peter Blazek 13, Cynoclub 14tr,
  S Duffett 20t, Thierry Maffeis 17, Michael Mattox 15,
  Clara Natoli 12b, Marc Pagani Photography 19t,
  Pandapaw 5t, Andrey Shadrin throughout,
  Ljupco Smokovski 21, Thomas Sztanek 16b
Map: Geoff Ward 4b

Every effort has been made to trace copyright holders and to obtain their permission for use of copyright material. The authors and publishers would be pleased to rectify any error or omission in future editions. All the Internet addresses given in this book were correct at the time of going to press. The author and publishers regret any inconvenience caused if addresses have changed or sites have ceased to exist, but can accept no responsibility for any such changes.

Library and Archives Canada Cataloguing in Publication

Gardner, Alison, 1981-
    Passport to Paris / Alison Gardner.

(Crabtree connections)
Includes index.
ISBN 978-0-7787-9955-9 (bound).--ISBN 978-0-7787-9977-1 (pbk.)

    1. Paris (France)--Juvenile literature. 2. Paris
(France)--Guidebooks--Juvenile literature. I. Title.
II. Series: Crabtree connections.

DC707.G37 2010   j944'.361   C2010-901517-7

Library of Congress Cataloging-in-Publication Data

Gardner, Alison, 1981-
  Passport to Paris / Alison Gardner.
      p. cm. -- (Crabtree connections)
  Includes index.
  ISBN 978-0-7787-9955-9 (reinforced lib. bdg. : alk. paper)
  -- ISBN 978-0-7787-9977-1 (pbk. : alk. paper)
  1. Paris (France)--Juvenile literature. I. Title. II. Series.

  DC707.G27 2010
  944'.361--dc22

                                        2010008061

Crabtree Publishing Company

Printed in the U.S.A./062010/WO20100815

Published in Canada
Crabtree Publishing
616 Welland Ave.
St. Catharines, Ontario
L2M 5V6

Published in the United States
Crabtree Publishing
PMB 59051
350 Fifth Avenue, 59th Floor
New York, New York 10118

Contents

Welcome to Paris

Paris is the capital city of France. This means that the **government** is based here. The people who live in Paris are called Parisians. Paris is a **historic** city with magnificent buildings that were built in the 17th century—more than 300 years ago!

My name is Jean-Paul, and I am going to show you around my city. I have lived here all my life. I love living in Paris because there is so much to see and do!

Paris

Stadium - Stade de France

La Défense Business Area

Disneyland Paris ➡

Champs-Élysées

Tuileries Garden
Louvre

Pompidou Centre

Eiffel Tower

River Seine

Notre Dame Cathedral

This map of Paris shows all the main attractions.

4

Green spaces

Despite all its buildings, Paris has many fine parks and open spaces. These range from the formal *Tuileries* Garden to the wilder *Bois de Boulogne* where Parisians and visitors can walk, cycle, ride horses, canoe, and fish. *Parc de la Villette* is Paris's largest open space, where you can go to concerts, movies, and plays. It is multicultural and always **festive**.

The *Tuileries* were built as royal pleasure gardens, filled with fruit and flowers.

City beach

For one month in the summer, sand is deposited along both sides of the River Seine. Known as the *Paris-Plages*, these artificial beaches are very popular. Beach chairs, shady palm trees, and temporary swimming pools make them cool havens in a hot, dusty city.

Did you know?
On average, 25 million **tourists** visit Paris every year.

Living in the City

A lot of people live in the center of Paris, so it is quite crowded. We have a large number of students and many foreign residents. Some people come to Paris to study and then decide to work here, because they like the Parisian life so much.

Places to live

Everyone needs a place to live and in Paris there are a lot of different types of homes. In the center of Paris there is not enough space for everyone to have a big house, so most people have apartments.

City views

Most of the apartments in the center of Paris are over 200 years old. My grandparents live in an old apartment. They have a balcony with a lot of plants and a really good view of the River Seine!

Living in a city apartment means you are close to all the stores and cafés.

Suburban living

In the **suburbs** of Paris, people live in houses. I live with my parents in a house in the suburbs. Out here, there are many backyards. In the center of Paris, houses with back yards are expensive. On the outskirts of Paris, tall buildings provide plenty of homes for the growing population.

Did you know?
Many people who live and work in Paris come from other countries, such as Algeria and Senegal.

Welcome to my home! I live in a house like the one above.

Going to a City School

I go to an elementary school in Paris. The French word for school is *école*. Our subjects are a lot like yours, but we also study English and Spanish from the age of five. This means that by the time we leave our *école* we are very good at languages! We also take lessons in **civic education**, which teaches us how to be good **citizens**.

Here are some children at my *école*.

Welcome to my school! It is called *École Charles de Gaulle*.

Secondary school

My sister Marie is older than me. She goes to a high school here in Paris. The French word for high school is *lycée*. Marie goes to a large *lycée* with more than 2,000 students! You can see her schedule below. On Wednesdays there are no classes, but the school is open for sports practice.

These students at the *lycée* are taking a break between their classes.

Monday	Tuesday	Wednesday
8a.m.—2p.m.	8a.m.—2p.m.	no classes
Thursday	**Friday**	**Saturday**
8a.m.—2p.m.	8a.m.—2p.m.	8a.m.—12 noon

Marie really enjoys going to the *lycée*, but they have a lot of homework to do. If she doesn't pass her exams in the summer, she is not allowed to move up a grade the following year. When she gets older, she is hoping to study art history at the famous Sorbonne University.

Did you know?
University education is free in France, but you must pass a very hard exam called the *baccalauréat* to be allowed to go.

Working in the City

Nearly everyone in the city goes to work—let me tell you about where my parents work.

There are 2.5 million people living and working in the city of Paris. Paris is an important world center for banks and other big businesses. *La Défense* is the business area of Paris. Many tourists go to see the 330 foot (100 m) high *Grande Arche* (an office building completed in 1989).

The *Grande Arche* is a huge squared arch that could cover *Notre Dame* **Cathedral**.

Did you know?
La Défense has 150,000 daily workers and is Europe's largest business district.

My mom works in an office building. She is a translator for an international company. This means she reads documents in French and then writes them out in English so that people from other countries can understand them.

The schools and hospitals in Paris need **skilled** people to work there. My dad works in a large hospital in Paris. He is a nurse and looks after patients in the Accident and Emergency department.

In the center of Paris many people have jobs in the **tourist industry**. This means that they help people visiting Paris from other countries.

A waiter in a Parisian restaurant serves tourists.

Getting Around the City

Paris is quite a small city, so it doesn't take long to get from one place to another.

The *Métro*

The *Métro* subway in Paris is quick and inexpensive. It reaches most areas of Paris and the suburbs. The time of day when everyone is going to work is called rush hour. The *Métro* gets very crowded during rush hour. The best way to travel on the *Métro* is with a *carnet*. This is a book of 10 tickets that costs 11 Euros (15 U.S. dollars). It is less expensive than buying separate tickets.

There are a lot of different ways to travel around Paris.

The Paris *Métro* has 368 stations.

River bus

The River Seine flows through Paris. The *bâteau* bus is a boat that travels up and down the river. It is slow and costs more than most other forms of transportation in Paris, so it is mainly tourists who use it.

A great way to explore Paris is on foot.

Cycling

Some people like to ride bicycles. Paris has a bicycle-sharing system called *Vélib*. People can rent a bicycle, which they pick up and drop off at one of the 750 **locations** in the city.

Walking

Paris has wide sidewalks and some roads that are closed to cars for most of the day. This makes Paris a pleasant place to walk around.

Did you know?
It only takes about two hours to walk across Paris.

Sightseeing in the City

The most well-known tourist attraction in Paris is the Eiffel Tower. It was finished in 1889 and was built to celebrate the anniversary of the **French Revolution**. From the top of the Eiffel Tower you can see that the city has been carefully planned. Wide, straight roads link many large squares together.

There are a lot of interesting sights in Paris. Let me show you around!

The Eiffel Tower was supposed to be a temporary structure, but it became so popular that it is still there 100 years later!

Did you know?
The Eiffel Tower has 1,665 steps and 20,000 light bulbs!

Victor Hugo saves *Notre Dame*!

The most famous cathedral in Paris is called *Notre Dame*. The cathedral is on an island in the middle of the River Seine. About 200 years ago the cathedral was falling down, so the city planners decided to destroy it. The French writer Victor Hugo really liked the cathedral. He wrote his book *The Hunchback of Notre Dame* to remind people that the cathedral was worth saving. His plan worked and the cathedral was repaired.

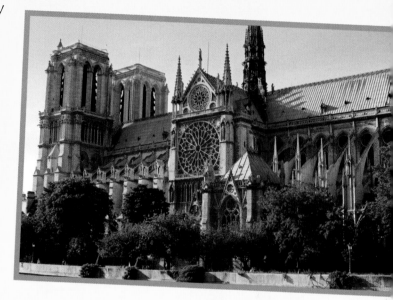

Disneyland

One of the most popular places is Disneyland Paris, located on the outskirts of the city. It is visited by people from all over the world.

Building work on *Notre Dame* Cathedral began in 1163. That's over 800 years ago!

Shopping in the City

Whatever you want to buy, you can find it in Paris! There are a lot of stores that sell different **products**.

What's in store?
The main shopping street in Paris is called the *Champs-Élysées*. Here the stores sell expensive items, such as jewelry and fashionable clothes. A lot of companies have their biggest stores on the *Champs-Élysées*.

In the center of Paris you will also find large **department stores** that sell a mixture of items such as food, clothes, toys, and shoes. The most famous department store in Paris is *Galeries Lafayette*.

Galeries Lafayette in Paris is 10 stories high and has 96 departments.

Shopping in Paris is great! There are hundreds of different stores from small street markets to huge department stores.

16

Books

If you enjoy books and magazines, bargains can be found at the secondhand book stalls that line the Left Bank of the River Seine.

Marvelous markets

Parisians enjoy visiting markets to buy their food and clothes. The markets are often in the suburbs of the city. At the food market all the food is fresh and comes from French farms. There you can buy seasonal fruit and vegetables, bread and cakes, cheeses, olives, garlic, and much more. At the **antique** markets you can buy beautiful old furniture, ornaments, and jewelry.

Parisians buy more food from markets than grocery stores.

Being Active in the City

Parisians are passionate about soccer! Paris held and won the World Cup final in 1998. A new **stadium** was built for the competition in the suburbs of the city. It is now used for cup final games and international games.

International ball games

Rugby is also a popular sport in Paris. The most successful Parisian team is called *Stade Français*. The French national team is very successful, too.

France won the soccer World Cup in 1998.

I am a fan of *Paris Saint-Germain*, a soccer team in Paris.

Watching the cyclists race up the Champs—Elysées is quite a spectacle.

Cycling and skating

French people also really enjoy cycling. Every year thousands of people line the streets of Paris to watch the *Tour de France*. This is a long bicycle race around the country that begins and ends in Paris.

Parisians are also crazy about roller-skating! Every Friday night 15,000 roller skaters skate round the center of Paris. Roads are closed so they can enjoy the wide, empty roads.

Did you know?
Many soccer players who play for *Paris Saint-Germain* are from other countries, including Brazil and Portugal.

Arts in the City

Paris has some of the most famous museums and art galleries in the world! Here you can see paintings and sculptures by well-known artists such as Monet and Leonardo da Vinci.

The *Louvre* was first opened to the public in 1793.

Museums

Most of the museums are in the historic center of Paris, near the river. This makes it easy for large numbers of people to get there.

> Today my grandparents are taking me to the biggest museum in France—the *Louvre*.

The *Louvre*

The *Louvre* is in a beautiful building. It used to be a royal palace. In 1988 a new entrance to the museum was built. It is a giant pyramid made of glass. It looks very different from the old building and some people were against it being built. I think it looks great! Inside, there are over 35,000 **exhibits** from all over the world.

The pyramid entrance to the *Louvre* is shown below.

Pompidou Centre

This cultural center is "inside out"—all its heating pipes, air ducts, and escalators are on the outside of the building! Inside are theaters, galleries, and a movie theater. The large square in front is like a stage for street performers who attract huge crowds on a fine day.

Glossary

antique Something that was made a long time ago

cathedral A large church

citizens People who live in a particular place

civic education Where you learn about your country and how it is run

department stores Large stores that sell a wide range of items

exhibits Paintings, sculptures, or objects in museums and art galleries

festive Fun event that takes place at certain times of the year

French Revolution The revolution in France against the royal family

government A group of people who are in charge of how a country is run

historic Something important from the past

locations Particular places

Métro Underground railway

products Items you can buy

skilled Experienced, trained well

stadium A large building that holds many people. Usually for soccer or other sports

suburbs The area of housing that surrounds a city

tourists Visitors to a city or place—often from other countries

tourist industry The businesses that help people visiting a city or place

Further Information

Web sites

The official Web site of the Paris Tourist Board can be found at:
http://en.parisinfo.com/

Visit the Eiffel Tower Web site at:
www.tour-eiffel.fr/teiffel/uk/index.html

Take a look at Disneyland Paris at:
http://us.disneylandparis.com/index.xhtml

Books

The Hunchback of Notre Dame by Victor Hugo, edited by Jan Needle. Walker Books (2006)

City Walks with Kids by Natasha Edwards and Roman Klonek. Universal Books (2008)

The Eiffel Tower by Meg Greene. Blackbirch Press (2003)

This is Paris by Miroslav Sasek. Universe Publishing (2004)

Index